PRAYER-PROOFING
YOUR
MARRIAGE

A Praying Wife's Devotional to Strengthen and
Protect Her Family

SHENEICO EASTWOOD

DAYELight
PUBLISHERS

ISBN: 978-1-958443-89-7 (paperback)

DEDICATION

This devotional is dedicated to every couple who has attended the Couples Getaway retreat.

This book is also dedicated to every wife who desires to have a better prayer life for her marriage and family.

Prayer is such a powerful tool, and accepting and practicing it will lead to greater and stronger marriages.

Through reading this book, I pray that you will develop stronger prayer habits and tap into the God-given power to bring forth the promises God has in store for your marriage.

ACKNOWLEDGMENTS

I thank God, who has given me this vision and seen me through the process.

I would like to express gratitude to my family, friends and loved ones who have encouraged me along the journey of writing this book.

Special thanks to my book coach, Crystal Daye of DayeLight Publishers, for assisting me along the journey of writing this book.

I express special appreciation to:

- My husband, Paul, who has been my constant rock.
- My friends, Dionne and Sherril, who would remind me to finish this book.
- My children, who are my greatest blessings.
- My prayer team from church: Andrea Gordon, Dorethea Stewart, Peteranne Donaldson, and KayeMarie Matthews, who stood with me in prayer throughout the process.

TABLE OF CONTENTS

INTRODUCTION

It is my pleasure to introduce you to *Prayer-Proofing Your Marriage: A Praying Wife's Devotional to Strengthen and Protect Her Family.* This has come at a time when the divorce rate is high, not just in Jamaica but across the world. I have seen where working marriages are not highlighted enough because people are more fixed on the failed ones. Prayer-proofing is here to help you safeguard your union and tap into your God-given ability to pray fervently for your marriage, spouse, children, and family.

My husband Paul and I have been married for eight years, and from year one, I knew that prayer would be key for our marriage to last and flourish. I learnt and practiced taking my concerns to the Lord before discussing them with my husband. I not only pray but also write my prayers down so I can go back to them later. I have accepted that God is the maker of my spouse and marriage and that He is the best person to turn to, as He already knows us and the plans He has for us.

Prayer works, and I can testify about that as many things we would have prayed about before and during our marriage have come to pass. We have experienced many answered prayers and many favour from God along this journey.

This task was given to me by God to share with the world some of the things they can pray about and the importance of keeping in prayer over your spouse, marriage, and family.

I write to every woman who has doubted the power of prayer. I write to encourage all wives to pray fervently for their husbands, marriage, and family. I write to let the world know that God has created marriage as a ministry, and we should constantly rely on Him to make our unions stronger, better, and wiser so it can be the light it was created to be.

1

LASTING LOVE

Above all, love each other deeply, because love covers over a multitude of sins. (1 Peter 4:8 – NKJV).

A lasting love in marriages doesn't just happen; as a couple, we must be deliberate about loving our spouse. Love is something we should express and show. We must ensure we are keeping each other entertained and interested in all areas of our marriages.

The Bible instructs us to love each other deeply and totally. Love is possible to last, but for this to happen, we should intentionally work together to make it happen. Love is a choice, and we should stand by the choice we made when we said "I do" to our partners. Loving our partner should not be based on our mood or if he or she does what we want, but we should love unconditionally, even when things are not going the way we would want them to. Practice being intentional about the love you show and give to your spouse.

Lord, we thank You in advance that our love will continue to burn… *(Continue writing your prayer):*

_____

_____

_____

_____

_____

_____

_____

_____

_____

_____

_____

_____

_____

_____

_____

_____

_____

_____

2

GODLY MARRIAGE

Therefore shall a man leave his father and his mother, and shall cleave unto his wife: and they shall be one flesh. (Genesis 2:24 – ASV).

As a couple, we should strive for our marriages to be Christ-like. Our marriages should represent Christ in all areas. Our love should be pure, patient, kind, and consistent. We must encourage ourselves daily and seek God to show us how our marriages can represent Him well.

Marriage was created for God, and as such, it should bring Him glory. Our marriages are not just for our personal pleasure or gain but to show God's love in a real and practical way.

May you choose to allow God to shine through your marriage to make it more like Him. I pray that we will understand that our union has caused us to become one and that we are one flesh. We should live each day becoming more like Christ and keep Him in the center. Our marriages should be a reflection of God's goodness, faithfulness, and love.

Father, I commit my marriage before You, and I pray it will represent Your love... *(Continue writing your prayer):*

_____

_____

_____

_____

_____

_____

_____

_____

_____

_____

_____

_____

_____

_____

_____

_____

_____

_____

3

MAKING YOUR MARRIAGE A MINISTRY

Be devoted to one another in love. Honor one another above yourselves. (Romans 12:10 – NIV).

As a married couple, your marriage is not just about you; it should be an example of Christ's love for the church. Our marriages should reflect Christ's love, grace, and purpose. We should aim to show Christ to others through the union we have with our spouse.

When people see your union, they should see Christ reflected in the way you live with each other. As a ministry, our marriage should serve us and others in a tangible way. We should keep in mind that God has called us to serve others above ourselves; this means if things aren't the way we desire, we should still serve our spouses the way we would want to be treated.

Today, I pray that you will allow God to show you how you can serve your spouse and how your marriage can be used as a ministry.

Lord, I pray that my marriage will reflect Christ and be an example to those who we encounter. I pray that... *(Continue writing your prayer):*

_____

_____

_____

_____

_____

_____

_____

_____

_____

_____

_____

_____

_____

_____

4

FAITHFULNESS

However, let each one of you love his wife as himself, and let the wife see that she respects her husband. (Ephesians 5:33 – ESV).

Loving your spouse also means being faithful to your spouse. We should aim to be faithful in our marriage, which is extremely important to create a lasting marriage. We should not only be faithful by not cheating sexually but also emotionally. Many times, people believe they didn't commit adultery because they didn't do the act of sex, but if you are getting connected to someone else emotionally, then you are playing a dangerous game. Faithfulness in all areas of your marriage will bear a fruitful union. Faithfulness is possible and, with God's help, attainable.

As couples, we should not put ourselves in a position to be tempted. We should flee the very appearance of sin. We should also be wise, open, and honest about our feelings to ourselves and our spouses. If you feel you are lacking, it is best to talk to your spouse instead of turning to the opposite sex for advice. As couples, we should guard our hearts and protect the union we vowed to. Today, ask the Lord to search your heart and reveal to you if you are lacking in this area. If you are faithful, ask God to help you remain this way and help you remain committed to each other.

Lord, please help us keep our minds, hearts, and intimate love for our spouses only. Help us to be aware of things that will cause us to get distracted and stray in the wrong direction. Please help us to look to You daily to keep us faithful and connected to our spouses.

Lord... *(Continue writing your prayer):*

_____

_____

_____

_____

_____

_____

_____

_____

_____

5

OUTSIDE INFLUENCE

Therefore, what God has joined together, let no one separate. (Mark 10:9 – NIV).

Couples sometimes make the mistake of allowing outsiders to get in between their unions. As couples, we should be careful who we allow to have a say in our marriage. Not everyone has our best interest at heart, and this can break the union. We should not turn to family or friends each time a situation arises but turn to each other and Christ. If things aren't being resolved, seek help from a professional or trusted friend with whom both parties are comfortable.

Too often, couples allow outside influence to create additional conflict in their marriages. Don't run to a person for help because you know they will say what you want to hear, but seek advice from persons who are fair and will give sound advice. Today, ask God to help you be wise regarding who you seek counsel from regarding your marriage and family.

Father, we ask for Your divine protection over our union and ask that we use wisdom to know who is for our marriage and who is not. We ask that we be intentional about those we let in and those we give a say to.

Lord, please help us to... (Continue writing your prayer):

_____

_____

_____

_____

_____

_____

_____

_____

_____

_____

_____

_____

_____

_____

_____

6

FORGIVENESS

Bearing with one another and, if one has a complaint against another, forgiving each other; as the Lord has forgiven you, so you also must forgive. (Colossians 3:13 – NIV).

Forgiveness is also a key ingredient in marriage; we must practice forgiving our spouses as we would want them to forgive us. Each spouse will mess up big or small at some point. We must be true to ourselves and forgive when this happens. We should also forgive quickly; let not the sun go down on your wrath.

Forgiveness will help mend things quickly and foster the rebuilding of trust. We all have sinned and fallen short of the glory of God. In the same way we would want God to forgive us, we must extend forgiveness to each other. Love holds no record of wrong, so as we forgive, we should also forget and not use past errors in new disagreements.

Forgiveness is not always easy, but it is possible with the help of God. If we struggle with this, we should seek God's help to overcome this hurdle.

Lord, I pray that we will forgive our spouse just as we want You to forgive us. Help us not to hold on to past hurt experienced by our spouse but to give each other grace so our marriage can flourish.

Lord, help us to… *(Continue writing your prayer)*:

_____

_____

_____

_____

_____

_____

_____

_____

_____

_____

_____

_____

7

OPENNESS

Ye know this, my beloved brethren. But let every man be swift to hear, slow to speak, slow to wrath. (James 1:19 – ASV).

In marriages, openness is very important as it facilitates trust. Couples should be open with each other to help them create that safe space. Being open will eliminate assumptions as you would have already known what is happening with each other.

Being open is a constant practice. It is not always easy, but the more you do it, the easier it becomes. Being open with your spouse is also a good way to build intimacy and growth in your relationship. Openness helps to enhance better communication and friendship in your union. Every couple should strive for this as it will create a better relationship. Today, ask God how you can become stronger in this area.

Lord, please help me to be open with my spouse. Help me to be honest about my feelings or what I am going through.

Lord, I pray that… *(Continue writing your prayer):*

_____

_____

_____

_____

_____

_____

_____

_____

_____

_____

_____

_____

_____

_____

_____

_____

8

TOGETHERNESS

Likewise, husbands, live with your wives in an understanding way, showing honor to the woman as the weaker vessel, since they are heirs with you of the grace of life, so that your prayers may not be hindered. (1 Peter 3:7 – ESV).

In a marriage, couples should understand that teamwork makes the marriage better. Couples should strive to work together and be on one accord. This will help to build a stronger union and allow for growth in the union.

Couples often live together, but they are living separate lives; therefore, you must be intentional about building a marriage where both partners work together and not against each other. Couples should realise that they are on the same team and operate in that truth. Today, ask God how you can practice togetherness in your union. Ask Him to hold you together with cords that cannot be broken.

Lord, I pray that my husband and I will work together in the various areas of our marriage. Lord, I pray that we will seek You to know how to build togetherness and unity.

Lord, I pray that… *(Continue writing your prayer):*

_____

_____

_____

_____

_____

_____

_____

_____

_____

_____

_____

_____

_____

_____

_____

_____

_____

9

HAPPINESS

A hot-tempered person stirs up conflict, but the one who is patient calms a quarrel. (Proverbs 15:18 – ESV).

Happiness is a choice, and we should choose to be happy with ourselves and our spouses. We should not rely solely on our spouses to make us happy; we should work together to create a happy marriage and home.

Happiness is attainable in marriage and certainly makes the home a lighter one. As couples, we should ensure that our homes foster happiness so each spouse can be comfortable and look forward to coming home. No one wants to come home to a home that is not joyful or peaceful. Each spouse should do their part to ensure that they are creating happy environments for their spouse and family.

Lord, we put our happiness before You and pray that we will seek You for guidance on how to truly be happy and contented in our marriage. We ask that You help us show love, kindness, and affection to our spouse, which in turn creates a safe space for each person to be truly happy.

Lord... *(Continue writing your prayer):*

_____

_____

_____

_____

_____

_____

_____

_____

_____

_____

_____

_____

_____

_____

_____

10

PEACE OF MIND

Do not be anxious about anything, but in everything by prayer and supplication with thanksgiving let your requests be made known to God. (Philippians 4:6 – ESV).

Peace of mind is important to keep each person calm and allow them to work better with each other. When an individual is uneasy in their thoughts, they become distracted or distant. Couples should learn how to relax more and not stress over the various situations they are faced with. They should practice playing with each other more and talking about situations they are facing to lighten the mood. Spouses who are at peace in their minds will relate better with each other.

Today, ask God to help you cast your cares upon Him and release any thoughts or cares that are causing you to be uneasy in your mind.

Father, I pray that my mind will be and stay at peace because I know the peacemaker. I pray that I will learn to trust in You and not worry but pray.

Lord, I pray that... *(Continue writing your prayer):*

_____

_____

_____

_____

_____

_____

_____

_____

_____

_____

_____

_____

_____

_____

_____

_____

_____

_____

11

HEALTH

Bless the Lord, O my soul, and forget not all his benefits, who forgives all your iniquity, who heals all your diseases, who redeems your life from the pit, who crowns you with steadfast love and mercy. (Psalm 103:2-4 – ESV).

Health is very important in a union; if either or both spouses are not well, this can strain the relationship. Health can affect all areas of the marriage, and it is key that we try as best as possible to keep in good health.

We also know that life is unpredictable, and we should constantly pray for our health and the health of our spouse. We should also recognize that if illness of any form should happen, we should support each other by standing with that spouse. Our vows said in sickness and health, so we are to be there for each other if sickness happens. We should also pray and ask God to give us the strength to go through as sickness takes patience, money, selflessness, and so much more that we are sometimes not able to give.

As someone who has been experiencing sickness a year after I got married, I can certainly say we have been tested. But I am so grateful that my spouse has been with me throughout this journey and has held me up in the lowest of times. My injury has affected many areas of my life, but having a supportive spouse has truly made the difference.

Lord, I pray that couples will look to You in sickness and health. I pray that You will grant couples what is needed to deal with a sick spouse. I pray that... *(Continue writing your prayer):*

_____

_____

_____

_____

_____

_____

_____

_____

_____

_____

_____

_____

12

WEALTH

But God will supply all your needs according to His riches in glory by Christ Jesus. (Philippians 4:19 – KJV).

Wealth is from God; we shouldn't feel bad for wanting it. We should also ensure that we want it for the right reasons. Without money, families cannot provide for their daily needs or even acquire things such as houses, cars, tuition for children, etc. Praying to be financially stable is okay, as this will help the couple take care of themselves and the home.

Couples should put their finances before God and work together to build wealth or become financially stable. Each couple will experience different financial struggles; however, they don't have to stay struggling, and working towards a better life is good. Couples must know that God is able to provide for their every need and that He is their source. Too often, we believe that we are our source or the job that we have but all things are from the Father.

Father, we pray that couples will find financial freedom through and in You. We pray that couples will use their God-given gifts to make room for themselves and their families. We ask that...
(Continue writing your prayer):

_____

_____

_____

_____

_____

_____

_____

_____

_____

_____

_____

_____

_____

_____

_____

_____

_____

13

PERSEVERANCE

Rejoice in hope, be patient in tribulation, be constant in prayer. (Romans 12:12 – ESV).

In life, we must know how to persevere. If we don't practice perseverance, then our marriages won't be able to last. We must be determined that we can make it and do what is required to make it. As couples, we must learn and practice perseverance, as this will cause our marriages to be successful.

Marriages are beautiful, but none is perfect. We all have good and bad days, but when the bad days come, we must ride it out together. We must ask God to strengthen our desire to push on the good and bad days. We must decide not to quit when things get rocky. We must do what is required to stick with each other. Perseverance is not easy, but it is worth it for couples to stay together.

We must also have our why and work on keeping it. Why did you get married? Why did you choose this person you are married to? Let the why motivate you to stay the course. Let the why and prayer be your strength in times of trouble.

Lord, I pray that I will choose to persevere for the sake of my marriage and family. I pray that You will give me the zeal needed to... *(Continue writing your prayer):*

_____

_____

_____

_____

_____

_____

_____

_____

_____

_____

_____

_____

_____

_____

_____

_____

_____

14

SEXUAL FULFILMENT

Let your fountain be blessed, and rejoice in the wife of your youth, a lovely deer, a graceful doe. Let her breasts fill you at all times with delight; be intoxicated always in her love. (Proverbs 5:18-19 – ESV).

Sex is healthy and is also a very important factor in marriage. We should aim to satisfy our spouses by having sex and ensuring that our spouse is satisfied. Sexual fulfillment is a need. If a spouse is not satisfied, it can cause problems in the marriage and even cause the unsatisfied spouse to look for satisfaction elsewhere.

As a wife and a husband, you must fulfill your spouse's sexual needs. This need should not be overlooked or treated lightly. Sexual fulfillment should also be discussed because you want to know that you are doing your part to satisfy your spouse. If there is a lack in this area, spouses should seek help so they can correct what has gone wrong.

Couples should pray about this area of their marriage, and ask God to keep them attracted and satisfied with each other. If each spouse aims to satisfy their partner, then this is the start. Sexual fulfillment is just as important as any other area in the marriage and should be treated as such.

Lord, I pray that You will help me to regard my spouse's sexual needs. Help me to satisfy my spouse sexually and... *(Continue writing your prayer):*

_____

_____

_____

_____

_____

_____

_____

_____

_____

_____

_____

_____

_____

15

SAFETY

He who dwells in the shelter of the most high will rest in the shadow of the Almighty. I will say of the LORD, "He is my refuge and my fortress, my God, in whom I trust." (Psalm 91:1-2 – NIV).

Everyone wants to know that they are safe and have a safe space. We should ensure that our spouses are safe in general from harm and danger and, spiritually, from the evil one. We should pray over our spouses for protection as they go out and come in daily. We should be very concerned about their safety and do what we can to make them feel safe.

Each spouse also needs to have compassion with each other. We should create a safe environment to ensure our spouses are comfortable letting down their guard around us. As a couple, we should be each other's safe space, where we can turn not just in trouble but also in the good times.

Today, try praying for the safety of your spouse and ask the Holy Spirit to lead you as you pray. Ask your spouse if they feel safe in general and safe in their relationship with you.

Lord, I pray for Your guidance as I pray for my spouse today. I pray that You will... *(Continue writing your prayer):*

_____

_____

_____

_____

_____

_____

_____

_____

_____

_____

_____

_____

_____

_____

_____

_____

16

PATIENCE

Love is patient and kind; love does not envy or boast; it is not arrogant or rude. It does not insist on its own way; it is not irritable or resentful. (1 Corinthians 13:4-5 – ESV).

Patience doesn't always come easily; this is something we have to work on daily. If you are struggling with this, you are not alone. Start practicing being patient with your spouse. If you need help, seek it, as everyone deserves to be shown grace and patience.

If we love others as ourselves, then we will exercise patience with each other. Just as you would want your spouse to be patient with you, you should also be patient with them. Try practicing patience daily. Pray and ask God to help you in this area. It is possible to be patient. We just need to be intentional about it; try taking that step today.

Father, You are patient God. I pray that You will help me in this area. I pray that… *(Continue writing your prayer):*

_____

_____

_____

_____

_____

_____

_____

_____

_____

_____

_____

_____

_____

_____

_____

_____

_____

_____

17

CHILDREN

Start children off on the way they should go, and even when they are old they will not turn from it. (Proverbs 22:6 – NIV).

C hildren are a gift and a heritage. If you have children, it is your duty to practice praying over them. Our children need our covering in prayer just as they need it in our provision. The Bible said we should suffer our children to come unto Him (see Matthew 19:14). It also said that we should train them in the way they should go, and when they are old, they will not depart from it. Start practicing teaching your children the Word of God, as this will keep them as they grow older. The world we live in is crazy, and our children have been significantly affected by the violence and abuse in our society. Be intentional about safeguarding your child with the Word of God.

Lord, I put my children before You. I pray that You will keep them safe from all harm at home, school, on the road, and at all times. I pray that my children will be blessed in every area of their lives and that Your Spirit of excellence will rest upon them. Lord, I pray that… *(Continue writing your prayer):*

_____

_____

_____

_____

_____

_____

_____

_____

_____

_____

_____

_____

_____

_____

_____

_____

_____

_____

_____

_____

18

INFERTILITY

and by faith even Sarah, who was past childbearing age, was enabled to bear children because she considered him faithful who had made the promise. (Hebrews 11:11 – NIV).

You may desire to be a parent and may experience delays. I pray that you will give that desire to the Lord and ask for His will to be done. As you do this, settle within yourself that whether God blesses you with children or not, you will give thanks to Him just the same. Our prayers are needed to activate God's plan for our lives, and they are also needed in the area of infertility. You should know that nothing is impossible with God, and He can bless you with a child—or children—even when the doctor says it is impossible.

As you pray for a baby, also pray that the baby will come full term and will live through labour and after. Too often, wives suffer from miscarriages and stillbirths. Be constant in prayer for your unborn child, and trust God to keep them safe.

Lord, children are from You, and I pray that You will bless me with a child if it is Your will. I pray that You will help me lift my faith and know that You can do what seems impossible to man.

Lord, I pray that… *(Continue writing your prayer):*

_____

_____

_____

_____

_____

_____

_____

_____

_____

_____

_____

_____

_____

_____

_____

_____

19

SUBMISSION

Wives, submit to your husbands, as is fitting in the Lord. (Colossians 3:18 – ESV).

Submission is a topic that many wives struggle with, but I pray you will submit to your spouse as it is fitting to the Lord. Seek the Lord for clarity and guidance to deal with submission. The Bible speaks about this; therefore, it is important to do this as the two become one. As you would want your husband to love you as Christ loves the church, you should also practice submission. We wives should ask God to guide our husbands as he leads. A husband guided by God will be easier to submit to. Submission is not agreeing with every decision your spouse will make. It is also not losing your voice but trusting your husband to lead and guide, and having the freedom to voice your opinions and ideas respectfully.

Lord, I pray for Your help to submit to my husband. I pray that You will guide me in knowing Your will. I pray that You will… *(Continue writing your prayer):*

20

GREAT COMMUNICATION

Know this, my beloved brothers: let every person be quick to hear, slow to speak, slow to anger. (James 1:19 – ESV).

Communication is a very important area in marriage. We should place great importance on this as it will make or break our union. Couples should prioritize this as without communication, your spouse will not be able to know what is going on in your head, and problems will not be solved. Communication also involves listening to your spouse to hear and understand what they are relating.

A marriage cannot grow if a spouse is not communicating properly or not communicating at all. Relationships start with communication and should continue to ensure that longevity takes place. Proper communication eliminates assumptions. As with everything else, we should seek God in this area as well to help us communicate stronger and more effectively and be better listeners.

Lord, I seek You as it relates to communicating with my spouse. Help me to be a better communicator and a better listener. Father, I pray that... *(Continue writing your prayer)*:

_____

_____

_____

_____

_____

_____

_____

_____

_____

_____

_____

_____

_____

_____

_____

_____

_____

21

SEXUAL PURITY

Let marriage be had in honor among all, and let the bed be undefiled: for fornicators and adulterers God will judge. (Hebrews 13:4 – ASV).

Even in marriage, sexual purity is important. As a married couple, it is important to keep your sexual thoughts and desires for your spouse only. We live in a world where promiscuity is promoted as the norm, but we have to know that sexual desires and acts are for your spouse only. We should feed our minds with things that are pure and of Christ. We should not allow the enemy to creep in and distract us with desires that are not Godly. Each couple is responsible for guarding their hearts, minds, and thoughts to keep them pure. The Lord called us to holiness and pureness, and we should strive for that, even in our marriage.

Purity in marriage enhances the relationship, but each person must put in the work to make it happen. Purity is your devotion to your spouse, loving them with all you have, not withholding any part of you. I pray that

God will keep you pure and committed to your spouse and give you the strength to stand, even when it seems hard.

Lord, I thank You that Your strength is perfect and that You are able to help me stay pure. I pray that... *(Continue writing your prayer):*

_____

_____

_____

_____

_____

_____

_____

_____

_____

_____

_____

_____

_____

_____

_____

22

FAVOUR

May the favour of the Lord our God rest on us; establish the work of our hands for us—yes, establish the work of our hands. (Psalm 90:17 – NIV).

Favour is from God, and He wants to establish His favour among His people. The Lord has great plans for us and our marriages, but we have to tap into those plans through prayer. We have to believe what God says He will do in our lives. We must speak it and live it. Favour is already upon us, but sometimes we operate defeated.

Today, I want you to speak favour over your life, marriage, and family. Favour is yours as a child of God, and sometimes we just need to walk into it. God wants to bless us and give us the desires of our hearts, but for this to happen, we have to walk and live like we know our inheritance. God's promises towards us are greater than what we have in store for ourselves and our relationships. Commit to walking in the favour of God and doing it together as a family.

Lord, I thank You for Your favour over my life. I thank You for wanting to bless me, and I received Your blessings.

Lord, I pray that… *(Continue writing your prayer):*

_____

_____

_____

_____

_____

_____

_____

_____

_____

_____

_____

_____

_____

_____

_____

_____

_____

_____

23

JOB SECURITY

"For I know the plans I have for you," declares the Lord, "plans to prosper you and not to harm you, plans to give you hope and a future." (Jeremiah 29:11 – NIV).

You may be struggling to secure a job to gain meaningful income for your family, but I speak release over you. Not earning a monthly income can be hard, as having a salary helps you provide for your family. I encourage you to remember that your job is not your source; God is. I encourage you to remember that He is your provider and will provide you with the right job to care for your needs. This could be through working for someone or using your God-given gift to make room for you.

The Lord has a plan and a purpose for your life; you need to seek Him to know what that plan is. You need to seek Him to direct your path and lead you to what you should be doing for work. Sometimes, we also have to work with what is available until we can do what we really want to do.

I pray that the Lord will bring you clarity as you seek Him. I pray that... *(Continue writing your prayer):*

_____

_____

_____

_____

_____

_____

_____

_____

_____

_____

_____

_____

_____

_____

_____

_____

_____

_____

_____

24

TRUST

Love bears all things, believes all things, hopes all things, endures all things. (1 Corinthians 13:7 – ESV).

Trust is a key ingredient in marriage. If trust is not present, then other issues will arise. Trusting your spouse is giving them the benefit of the doubt that what they say and do is true. If you are not able to believe your spouse or have faith in their word, then this will certainly break down the relationship. Lack of trust is not healthy and should be worked on as soon as it is identified. We also have to accept that trust is earned, so if this trust has been broken, the partner who has broken it should do what is needed to earn back their spouse's trust. Each partner must also extend grace, which helps both partners to forgive and move on from mistrust.

Trusting your spouse means having faith in them to know they will hold to their vows and word. If you struggle with trusting your partner, you must be open and honest about it. You must also seek the required help to fix the situation to improve your marriage.

Lord, I pray that trusting my spouse will be easy. I pray that You will remove every doubt that would want me to believe otherwise about my partner.

Lord, I pray that... *(Continue writing your prayer):*

_____

_____

_____

_____

_____

_____

_____

_____

_____

_____

_____

_____

_____

_____

_____

_____

_____

25

GRACE

> *But he gives more grace. Therefore it says, "God opposes the proud but gives grace to the humble." (James 4:6 – ESV).*

We all need grace. God gives us grace daily because we all have sinned and fallen short. Giving grace to our spouse is important for healing and restoration. We should forgive quickly and move past disagreements to build a stronger and better marriage.

Grace should be given as often as it is required. We must be humble enough to know that our spouse will not always get it right or even do what we expect of them. But we should not hold it against them but exercise grace one toward another. Extending grace is giving your spouse another chance to get it right or make it better. We should also acknowledge when our spouse is making an effort to fix things.

Without grace, we are saying that we can't forgive and move past what was done. This certainly will not help the union. If we want our marriage to work, we have to see grace as important and necessary for it to function. Someone gave you a second chance, so you should also give your spouse a second chance to make things better.

Lord, I need Your help in this area. Please help me to extend grace when it is needed. Lord, please... *(Continue writing your prayer):*

_____

_____

_____

_____

_____

_____

_____

_____

_____

_____

_____

_____

_____

_____

26

SUPPORTIVENESS

As Sarah obeyed Abraham, calling him lord. And you are her children, if you do good and do not fear anything that is frightening. (1 Peter 3:6 – ESV).

L ove is also supporting your spouse. If you care about your spouse, then you should support their dreams and desires. You should be your spouse's cheerleader when they are working towards a dream. Support should be given, even without asking. We have to be that spouse who believes in their partner. We should be there for them, not just in words but also physically. It may be staying up with them while they are working on a project or assisting with housework when they have other important tasks to work on. Support should be given, even if it is not being reciprocated. As couples, we shouldn't practice tit for tot. Treat your spouse how you would want to be treated.

Supporting your spouse means being there for them in times of need and otherwise. Put into practice supporting your spouse, and it will become easier, even though we shouldn't see it as a great task. Love gives, love supports, and love stands with. I pray that God will work on our hearts to do better in this area.

Lord, I thank You that You are a God who is able to help us make our marriages stronger and better. I pray that… *(Continue writing your prayer):*

_____

_____

_____

_____

_____

_____

_____

_____

_____

_____

_____

_____

_____

_____

_____

_____

27

FINANCES

Jabez cried out to the God of Israel, "Oh, that you would bless me and enlarge my territory! Let your hand be with me and keep me from harm so that I will be free from pain." And God granted his request. (1 Chronicles 4:10 – AMP).

God is interested in all areas of our lives and marriages. This means He is concerned about our finances. Let us speak increase in our finances. Life can be challenging, especially when we can't meet our daily needs. Let us keep in prayer over our finances as couples and ask God to sustain us where there is a lack. May He open the windows of heaven and bless us in this area. I pray that He will help us to be wise as He blesses us to bless others. I pray that our borders will be enlarged financially.

Lack of money can strain a marriage. Each partner should do their part to ease this burden. Couples should also come to a mutual agreement on how the monthly expenses will be handled. Couples should work together to create and make good financial choices. While praying about your finances is important, we must be practical about it and develop good saving habits.

Lord, I thank You that all things are from You, including money. I pray that You will bless my family and enlarge our territory. I pray that... *(Continue writing your prayer)*:

_____

_____

_____

_____

_____

_____

_____

_____

_____

_____

_____

_____

_____

_____

_____

28

IN-LAWS

For this reason a man shall leave his father and his mother, and shall be joined to his wife; and they shall become one flesh. (Genesis 2:24 – AMP).

A s a married couple, the Bible says we should leave our mother and father and be joined as one flesh, but this doesn't mean we shouldn't have a good relationship with our in-laws. We should strive to have a respectable relationship with our spouses' parents and family. The Bible says as much as possible we should live at peace with everyone (see Romans 12:18). A good relationship with our in-laws is great for the family and will enhance our relationship with our spouse. If you are trying your best to be at peace and it is not working, we should then try to be civil with each other. We should also pray and ask God to help us in this area.

For couples who have a good relationship with their in-laws, they should not take it for granted but pray that it will continue this way. Each spouse should also try to encourage the bond between their parents and spouse. Relationship building is not always easy, but it is surely possible. Praying about your in-laws before you know them is also a good place to start.

Lord, I pray that You will help make relationships between in-laws and spouses great. I pray that a strong bond will be created among them and that they will be... *(Continue writing your prayer):*

_____

_____

_____

_____

_____

_____

_____

_____

_____

_____

_____

_____

_____

_____

_____

29

INFIDELITY

Marriage is to be held in honor among all [that is, regarded as something of great value], and the marriage bed undefiled [by immorality or by any sexual sin]; for God will judge the sexually immoral and adulterous. (Hebrews 13:4 – AMP).

Infidelity does not have to be your reality. You can love one wife or one husband until death do you part. You don't have to fall into the trap of cheating on your spouse. As much as possible, try to stick to your spouse only. This means running from temptation like Joseph. Don't set yourself up by saying you are strong enough or this can't happen to you. To ensure this doesn't happen, you should stay clear of situations that will cause you to fall.

Don't look for trouble, but stay close to God, who can sustain you and keep you from falling. Infidelity is common in marriage. You must be determined to stay faithful. Being faithful takes a daily choice. But what if you should fall into this situation? Grace can be given because it is possible to recover from infidelity and build back stronger than before.

Couples should be practical concerning infidelity to know that they should not put themselves in a position for this to take place. Couples should be accountable to each other and open about what they are feeling. I pray that you will not fall into this trap but you will choose to be faithful to your spouse no matter what.

Father, I thank You that Your strength is perfect in my weakness. I pray that You will give me the strength I need to stay faithful. I pray that... *(Continue writing your prayer):*

_____

_____

_____

_____

_____

_____

_____

_____

_____

_____

30

WISDOM

For the LORD gives [skillful and godly] wisdom; From His mouth come knowledge and understanding... (Proverbs 2:6 – AMP).

Wisdom comes from God, and anyone who lacks wisdom should ask Him. Wisdom is needed and important in marriages; it helps us make rational decisions and deal with situations that may arise wisely. Wisdom directs our choices and guides us in the right direction.

If wisdom is lacking in our decision-making, we tend to make the wrong decisions or act out of emotions. Wisdom, when used the right way, will build stronger unions and stronger families. Wisdom will guide us to be better and do better for our relationship.

Making wise choices will save a marriage in all areas and make both spouses more comfortable knowing that their spouse operates in wisdom. Being wise in how you deal with the affairs of your marriage will create a stronger family and union. It will help you care for and guide your children. Let us commit to operating in wisdom to enhance our relationships and family life.

Father, I seek You for wisdom in my daily life. I pray that You will help me to be wise in Your eyes. Lord, I pray that... *(Continue writing your prayer):*

_____

_____

_____

_____

_____

_____

_____

_____

_____

_____

_____

_____

_____

_____

_____

_____

31

HEALING FROM THE PAST

Bless the Lord, O my soul, and forget not all his benefits, who forgives all your iniquity, who heals all your diseases. (Psalm 103:2-3 – ESV).

Let go and let God heal and restore you. You can't change the past, and hanging on to past hurts will not help you or your current relationship. Healing comes from God, and He wants us to be whole. If you have not let go of hurts from your past, then this is something you need to work on urgently. Hanging on to past hurt will stop you from receiving the love your spouse is giving you. Not letting go of past hurt will cause you to build a shield to protect yourself, and this can cause serious damage to the family you are now building.

Learn to forgive yourself and those who have hurt you. Release yourself from guilt, shame, or disappointment so you can freely accept the good thing you now have with your spouse. Not everyone will hurt you. Not everyone will have the wrong motive, but you will have to trust what your spouse brings to the table. Trust that God has blessed you and provided you with a better life and a better spouse. Walk in the freedom God has given you, and know that you are healed.

Lord, I thank You that there is nothing we face that is greater than You. I pray that You will heal broken hearts and past wounds. I pray that... *(Continue writing your prayer):*

_____

_____

_____

_____

_____

_____

_____

_____

_____

_____

_____

_____

_____

_____

32

UNITY

Make every effort to keep the unity of the Spirit through the bond of peace. (Ephesians 4:3 – NIV).

It is so important to build a relationship that fosters unity. Why wouldn't you want to have a unified union? As couples, we should strive for peace in our homes. A unified home is welcoming and creates a good atmosphere for great things to happen. Working together to maintain unity will spill over into how strong your marriage will become.

If you want a strong, healthy marriage, commit to being peaceful toward your spouse. Bite your tongue if you must, as it can lead you to say the wrong thing. No one wants to come home to a nagging spouse or a heavy environment. Relationships don't have to be as hard and complicated as we make them. We should pray and seek God's help to keep our marriage and family united.

Are you struggling to be unified with your spouse? Stop and assess what is happening. Pray and ask God to lead you in creating unity in your relationship and family. Commit daily to keeping the peace because prayer without work will not bring forth results.

Lord, I thank You that peace comes from You, and that You are able to help me live in unity with my spouse and family. Lord, I pray that... *(Continue writing your prayer):*

_____

_____

_____

_____

_____

_____

_____

_____

_____

_____

_____

_____

_____

_____

_____

33

RESPECT

However, each one of you also must love his wife as he loves himself, and the wife must respect her husband. (Ephesians 5:33 – NIV).

A marriage that doesn't have respect will be a problematic one. Each spouse should show and give respect to their spouse. Respecting your spouse will eliminate unnecessary arguments and tension. Respect is one of the key needs for the male, and it makes them feel appreciated and honoured when this is shown. Respect is also important to the wife as she will feel safe and secure when this is given. Just as you would want to feel respected, you should also give it freely to your spouse. In marriages, we tend to hold back based on what we don't receive, but we should break that cycle.

Respect is not doubting the capacity for change, lowering your standard, or accepting bad behaviour but believing that your spouse can change, encouraging and showing grace, and working together to fulfill God's vision for your marriage.

Respect is letting your spouse know they are valued and loved.

Lord, I thank You for giving me the capacity to respect and love my spouse as You have called me to do. I pray that You will help me to show respect to my spouse daily in word and deed. I pray that... *(Continue writing your prayer):*

_____

_____

_____

_____

_____

_____

_____

_____

_____

_____

_____

_____

_____

_____

34

SELF-CONTROL

> *Rather, he must be hospitable, one who loves what is good, who is self-controlled, upright, holy and disciplined. (Titus 1:8 – NIV).*

Self-control is needed in marriage to keep the relationship strong, even when faced with challenges. Practicing self-control is being mindful of how your reaction will impact your spouse. One should love and respect their spouse enough to operate with self-control and give the patience that is needed for this to happen. If we cannot practice self-control, then we have serious problems that will impact our spouse and family negatively. We should be able to control our emotions and not react in any form that will hurt or harm our loved ones.

Love is selfless and requires us to be intentional in how we respond to situations and how we treat the ones we love. We should be slow to anger and look toward creating peace in all situations. We will get upset, but how we respond will make the difference. Choose self-control in how you relate to your spouse and watch how things will be different in your marriage. Prayer is key to making this possible; the greatest thing is that all things are possible with God.

Father, we look to You, the one who is able to do all things. I put my marriage before You and ask that You help me practice self-control. Help me to think before I respond. Help me to... *(Continue writing your prayer):*

_____

_____

_____

_____

_____

_____

_____

_____

_____

_____

_____

_____

_____

_____

35

PROTECTION OVER YOUR MARRIAGE AND FAMILY

He will cover you with his feathers, and under his wings you will find refuge; his faithfulness will be your shield and rampart. (Psalm 91:4 – NIV).

We should not take the safety and security of our families for granted. We must pray daily for our marriage and families that God will protect us and keep us safe from all harm and danger. We live in a world filled with evil, and we must keep ourselves covered from all that can happen. Protection is needed when we travel on the road, when our children go to school or work, and when we are at home. Constant protection is needed from all who want to see your relationship and family fail. It is needed from all the traps the enemy will set to break down our union. At times, protection is needed from us so we can operate in the will of God.

Life will come with different challenges, but there is no challenge that we will face that God cannot protect us from. God is able to keep us safe and covered as He is our refuge and hiding place. We have to trust God to shield us from all harm that will come our way.

Lord, I thank You for covering us under Your wings. We thank You for Your angels encamping around us. I pray that You will… *(Continue writing your prayer):*

_____

_____

_____

_____

_____

_____

_____

_____

_____

_____

_____

_____

_____

_____

_____

_____

_____

36

AMBITIOUS SPOUSE

In all labour there is profit, but idle chatter leads only to poverty. (Proverbs 14:23 – NLV).

Every spouse should be ambitious in wanting a good life and a good marriage. A lazy spouse will not make those dreams a reality. The Bible says that by the sweat of our brows, we will eat bread (see Genesis 3:19), which confirms that we should have ambition and work towards achieving goals for our marriage and families. If you or your spouse is lacking in this area you should seek God for a refreshing in purpose and ambition. We should not settle and be comfortable in lack, but work towards achieving a better life for each other to be comfortable. Ambition is needed by the wife as much as it is needed for the husband. Both the husband and wife should be ambitious enough to want to grow together in their relationship and also in their professional life.

Strategizing by writing down your goals and vision as a couple is important. Planning ahead and working on those plans is key to having a successful marriage. Ambition will take compromise and great communication to make your plans work. Don't settle with being lazy; build your ambition by building your self-confidence and strengthening your desire for better.

Father, I seek You today and ask for Your help in helping me become more ambitious. This will help my marriage to grow and help me attain my goals. Father, I pray that my spouse will also develop the quality of being ambitious as we build together. I pray for Your guidance and direction. I pray for... *(Continue writing your prayer):*

_____

_____

_____

_____

_____

_____

_____

_____

_____

_____

37

ADDICTION

Therefore, submit to God. Resist the devil and he will flee from you. (James 4:7 – NKJV).

Having an addiction is not a good thing and can cause the breakdown of the marriage and family. If you or your spouse are struggling in this area, we believe with you for deliverance. You may be addicted to alcohol, drugs, porn, or anything else that is causing you to act negatively or harmfully toward yourself or others. Breaking addiction is possible, but we must be intentional about getting the help that is needed. Resist the devil and those things you are addicted to. God can deliver you or your spouse from this and restore you to a better way of life for yourself and your family.

You don't have to be a slave to addiction. You have the power to break free. Fight with all your might and remove yourself from the place or space that causes you to fall into this trap. This could mean changing friends or changing what you watch or listen to. This could also mean developing a stronger relationship with God.

Father, I put before You every spouse who struggles with addiction. I ask for Your healing and deliverance. I pray that You will set them free from that which holds them hostage.

Lord, I pray that… *(Continue writing your prayer):*

_____

_____

_____

_____

_____

_____

_____

_____

_____

_____

_____

_____

_____

_____

_____

38

BITTERNESS

Let all bitterness, wrath, anger, clamor and evil speaking be put away from you, with all malice. (Ephesians 4:31).

Have you ever been bitter against someone or something? Have you experienced someone being bitter with you? It is certainly not a good feeling. Bitterness is often caused by unforgiveness and unresolved issues. The great thing is that we can choose not to continue being bitter toward our spouse or family. We can overcome bitterness through forgiveness and extending grace. What does it profit you or your relationship to continue in bitterness? We all should aim for a healthier relationship, and one way to attain this is by letting go of hurt and allowing God's life to fill our hearts.

If you want your marriage to last and flourish in all areas, you have to be deliberate about what you allow to impact you or your union. Communicate when you are hurt so your spouse is aware and can get the opportunity to fix things. Don't allow things to fester until bitterness takes you over. Instead, look to God, who is your maker and the maker of your spouse, to make things better.

Dear Lord, I know I can trust You to help me out of this situation and to make me better and not bitter. I pray that my spouse and I will not entertain bitterness but we will show grace and love towards each other. Lord, I pray... *(Continue writing your prayer):*

_____

_____

_____

_____

_____

_____

_____

_____

_____

_____

_____

_____

_____

_____

39

UNSAVED SPOUSE

Wives, in the same way submit yourselves to your own husbands so that, if any of them do not believe the word, they may be won over without words by the behavior of their wives. (1 Peter 3:1 – NIV).

Many wives struggle with their husbands not coming to Christ, and this can sometimes put a strain on the relationship based on differences in beliefs. If you are currently experiencing this situation, I encourage you to stay fervent in prayer and trust God to call him unto Himself. I also encourage you to let the way you live be that example of Christ. You must ensure that there is no double standard in how you relate to your spouse at home. Your life should reflect Christ in every area so he will see Christ in you and want to serve the God you serve.

It is our responsibility as wives to balance ministry and our relationship with our spouse. We should ensure that we are practical in serving our spouse and making time for their needs. We should ensure that we are not just going to church, participating in all the activities, and not leaving any time to spend with our spouse. Also, invite your spouse to church activities, not just Sunday or Saturday morning services. Do not lose hope because no one is beyond the reach of God.

Lord, I pray for unsaved spouses. I pray that Your Holy Spirit will work on their hearts and draw them to You. I pray that... *(Continue writing your prayer):*

_____

_____

_____

_____

_____

_____

_____

_____

_____

_____

_____

_____

_____

_____

_____

COMMITMENT

May your fountain be blessed, and may you rejoice in the wife of your youth. (Proverbs 5:18 – NIV).

Staying committed to your spouse is a daily choice. It is not based on feelings but on facts. You have to know what you know and operate off that. Commitment to your spouse and family is important for your marriage to last, even on the bad days, even on the days when you are faced with a financial challenge or a health challenge.

Loving and being committed to your spouse shouldn't change based on weight gain or a change in financial status. As a couple, the goal should be to love and honour your spouse through thick or thin, better or worse, and in sickness and health. This is the vow you made on your wedding day. Life and people will change, but both spouses should remember the why and stick with that.

Commitment in marriage is similar to our commitment to God; we don't turn from God when

He doesn't give us the answer we need or when we face adversity, but we use those times to pull closer to Him. It is the same for our relationship with our spouse; we use the good times to build and the rough times to hold on to what we have built. We don't lose commitment to our spouse because of aging, but we love the person totally despite any physical changes. Choose to stay committed to the one you said I do to. Pray constantly for God to renew your love daily, and work on keeping the flames burning.

Today, I pray that God will ignite the fire of love and keep me committed and attracted to my spouse. I pray that God will… *(Continue writing your prayer):*

_____

_____

_____

_____

_____

_____

_____

_____

_____

_____

10 TIPS TO BUILD A BETTER PRAYER LIFE WITH YOUR SPOUSE

1. Do a prayer board together.
2. Take prayer walks.
3. Fast together.
4. Attack the problem and not each other.
5. Make and keep Jesus at the center of your union.
6. Forgive quickly.
7. Exercise grace toward your spouse.
8. Do daily devotion together.
9. Pray frequently as a family.
10. Keep the lines of communication open.

ABOUT THE AUTHOR

Sheneico Eastwood has been a Christian for over twenty years and is passionate about God and young people. She has worked with young persons through different youth ministries and through the visitation of children's homes. Her new venture and passion is to reach out to single mothers and share her experiences to help them along the way. She shares this not only through words but also through deeds, as practical love is needed in today's society.

She is a wife and a mother of three beautiful children. She is the youth director at the Portmore Church of God, part owner and director of P&S Events and Vacations, where she organizes vacation deals and hosts marriage retreats and events with her husband, Paul. She is the author of the book **Never Gems: 70 Lessons I Learnt Along The Way.**

Sheneico is a graduate of the University of the West Indies, Mona, where she gained a bachelor of arts degree in library and information studies with a minor in literacy studies.

AUTHOR INVITATION

God has a way of using what we call mistakes and errors to make something beautiful and something of higher value. If you are having a hard time accepting who you are, seek God and watch Him turn things around for you.

Connect with Sheneico Eastwood via Instagram @ thecouplesgetaway and sheneicoeastwoodminitries

Sheneico is thrilled about speaking at your next couple's ministry or retreat, couples or women's conference, group meetings, and/or seminars. Please send an invitation to eastwoodsheneico@gmail.com

Bulk order discounts are available for churches, women's ministries, associations, and others. To place your order, you may use the email address above.

www.ingramcontent.com/pod-product-compliance
Lightning Source LLC
LaVergne TN
LVHW051812080426
835513LV00017B/1926